Pebble® Plus

LET'S LOOK AT COUNTRIES

WORLD of SCIENCE

LET'S LOOK AT
CANADA

BY JOY FRISCH-SCHMOLL

CAPSTONE PRESS
a capstone imprint

Pebble Plus is published by Capstone Press,
1710 Roe Crest Drive, North Mankato, Minnesota 56003
www.mycapstone.com

Library of Congress Cataloging-in-Publication Data
Names: Frisch-Schmoll, Joy, author.
Title: Let's look at Canada / by Joy Frisch-Schmoll.
Description: North Mankato, Minnesota : Capstone Press, 2019. | Series: Pebble plus. Let's look at countries
Identifiers: LCCN 2018029936 (print) | LCCN 2018031714 (ebook) | ISBN 9781977103901 (eBook PDF) | ISBN 9781977103819 (hardcover) | ISBN 9781977105608 (pbk.)
Subjects: LCSH: Canada—Juvenile literature.
Classification: LCC F1008.2 (ebook) | LCC F1008.2 .F75 2019 (print) | DDC 971—dc23
LC record available at https://lccn.loc.gov/2018029936

Editorial Credits
Erika L. Shores, editor; Juliette Peters, designer; Jo Miller, media researcher;
Laura Manthe, production specialist

Photo Credits
Dreamstime: Ivansabo, 17; iStockphoto: Lijuan Guo, 14, stockstudioX, 13; Shutterstock: Ami Parikh, 22-23, 24, BGSmith, 9, Brent Hofacker, 19, Chase Dekker, Cover Bottom, , Cover Back, Globe Guide Media Inc, 3, Globe Turner, 22 (Inset), Helen Filatova, 21, Matthew Jacques, 7, nate, 4, Russ Heinl, Cover Top, Sergei Bachlakov, 11, SF photo, 5, Stas Moroz, Cover Middle, Sylvie Bouchard, 8, Xuanlu Wang, 1, Zoran Karapancev, 15

Note to Parents and Teachers

The Let's Look at Countries set supports national curriculum standards for social studies related to people, places, and culture. This book describes and illustrates Canada. The images support early readers in understanding the text. The repetition of words and phrases helps early readers learn new words. This book also introduces early readers to subject-specific vocabulary words, which are defined in the Glossary section. Early readers may need assistance to read some words and to use the Table of Contents, Glossary, Read More, Internet Sites, Critical Thinking Questions, and Index sections of the book.

Printed and bound in China.
970

TABLE OF CONTENTS

Where Is Canada?

Canada is the largest country in North America. It borders the United States. It touches three oceans. The capital city is Ottawa.

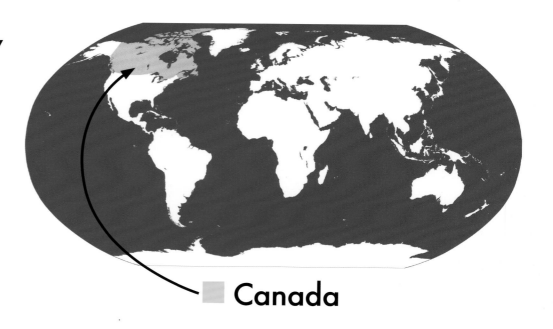

Canada

Ottawa, Canada

From Forests to Tundra

Canada has forests, mountains, and prairies. In the far north, the tundra is flat. Few trees grow there. Winters are very cold.

In the Wild

Grizzly bears and moose feed on plants. Wolves hunt for elk. Beavers swim in streams. Polar bears look for seals on arctic ice.

beaver

grizzly bear

People

The first Canadians were First Nations people. Then others came from France and England. Today Canada is a country of many cultures. Most people live in the south.

On the Job

Most Canadians work in stores, offices, and hospitals. Others have jobs in schools. Some make cars in factories. Fishers catch salmon. Loggers cut down trees.

Celebrating Canada

Canada Day is July 1. It celebrates the country's birthday. There are parades, concerts, and fireworks. Police officers called Mounties ride horses in a musical show.

On the Ice

Ice hockey is the most popular sport in Canada. Canadians learn to ice skate when they are young. Every town has an ice rink and a hockey team.

At the Table

Canadians eat a lot of meat and seafood. Poutine is a popular food. It is french fries covered with cheese and gravy.

Famous Site

Horseshoe Falls is the largest waterfall at Niagara Falls. Water rushes over the edge. Mist fills the air. Boat rides give people a close look.

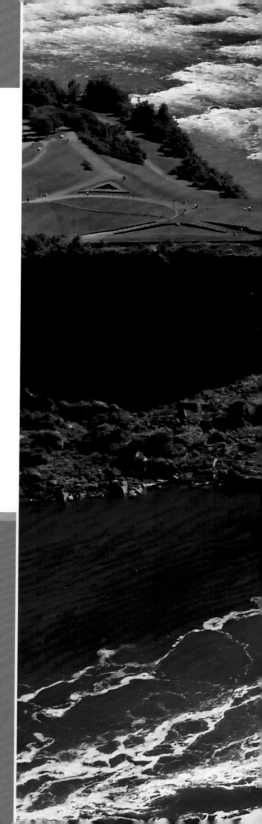

QUICK CANADA FACTS

Canadian flag

Name: Canada
Capital: Ottawa
Other major cities: Toronto, Montreal, Vancouver
Population: 35,623,680 (2017 estimate)
Size: 3,855,103 square miles (9,984,670 sq km)
Language: English, French
Money: Canadian dollar

GLOSSARY

arctic—the area around the North Pole where it is very cold

border—the line between two countries

culture—the way of life, ideas, customs, and traditions of a group of people

First Nations—native people who lived in Canada before European explorers arrived

logger—a worker who cuts down trees to make lumber and paper

Mounties—members of the Royal Canadian Mounted Police, the national police force of Canada

salmon—a large fish with pink flesh

tundra—a large, open plain in an arctic area where the ground is always frozen

READ MORE

Mara, Wil. *Canada.* Enchantment of the World. New York: Scholastic, 2018.

Markovics, Adam. *Canada.* Countries We Come From. New York: Bearport Publishing, 2017.

Pang, Guek-Cheng. *Canada.* Cultures of the World. New York: Cavendish Square Publishing, 2015.

INTERNET SITES

Use FactHound to find Internet sites related to this book.

Visit *www.facthound.com*

Just type 9781977103819 and go.

Check out projects, games and lots more at
www.capstonekids.com

CRITICAL THINKING QUESTIONS

1. What parts of Canada would you like to visit? What things would you pack for your trip?

2. Many arctic animals have thick, white fur. How does this help them?

3. Describe how Canadians celebrate Canada Day.

INDEX